Beginner's Guide to Your First Handgun

by Keith R. Baker

The Beginner's Guide to Your First Handgun

**Copyright 2015 by Keith R. Baker
All Rights Reserved**

Dedication

This guide is dedicated to all those helpful shooters who have led the way and contributed to the present level of knowledge and understanding of firearms available.

Also to those currently among us who share their knowledge even as they press forward to increase and expand it.

Finally to those eager souls coming along in the wake of the above two groups. May you always be alert, vigilant and armed.

Keith R. Baker, Ronan, Montana USA
2015

The Beginner's Guide to Your First Handgun

Table of Contents

Forward

Selection and Purchase of Your First Handgun

Handling Your First Handgun

Ammunition - The Good, the Bad and the Ugly

Safety First, Foremost and Always

Shooting Your First Handgun

Maintaining, Cleaning and Storing

Forward

About the Author

To begin with you should know a few things about me, the author. I am not a gun dealer nor retailer of firearms nor accessories. Nor am I a gunsmith. I am a shooter.

My opinions are my own and have been earned through a lifetime of owning, using, shooting, cleaning guns and teaching those things to others. I am an NRA Certified Pistol Instructor and Chief Range Safety Officer (among other things) and first fired a handgun at the age of 8. That was more than 50 years ago. How many years more than 50? Does that really matter?

Depending upon **your definition of expert** either I am one or not. Your definition, all right? Not mine. The US Navy seemed to think that I was a Rifle Expert and Pistol Expert a few decades ago. I'm not sure my definition of Expert and the Navy's would agree anymore. I guess the point being that there are things you may be able to gain from reading this at a cover price that should make sense for the advice you are receiving.

Why I wrote this guide. It's 2015 and the topic of gun ownership is at a fever pitch in the US and elsewhere around the globe. Folks are buying guns and learning to shoot in

The Beginner's Guide to Your First Handgun

record numbers. <u>Hooray.</u> Many of these newcomers are getting bad advice and inferior instruction and don't have someone reliable to help them. <u>Booo.</u> So this is for those people because I understand their need and hope to at least partially fill it.

What this book is and is not...

This is written for beginners, newbies, novices or those who've been away from guns for an extended period. If you are not in that list, this may not be the book for you. The idea here being to help with the safe selection, acquisition, handling, firing, maintaining, cleaning, storing and carrying-for-personal-protection one or more handguns. Ammunition selection and acquisition are also discussed.

This is **not** an encyclopedic tome of great depth intended to cover all handguns for all time and for all applications. It is written in the United States of America in 2015 and intended for folks living in that country. Specific availability of various guns and ammunition mentioned herein will vary considerably depending upon the location of the user.

Which brings me to the next point - namely, this is not an exhaustive discussion of regulations and laws pertaining to the possession and use of guns in each state, county, city, village, etc., and Yes, such things exist in some places. General comments contained herein about those topics may be helpful as guides and are thus included. They are not substitutes for researching the particular requirements of the law where you live.

There are many books with much more in-depth information available; this is a primer for the described audience. Many shooters in this world have greater depth than mine. If they have written something, you might want to read that too. If they haven't written anything, what difference does their knowledge and experience make?

The Beginner's Guide to Your First Handgun

Readers are encouraged to further their own knowledge from such publications that appeal most to their own personal tastes and purposes. Just be careful when choosing your sources - not all are good.

The Beginner's Guide to Your First Handgun

The Selection and Purchase of Your First Handgun:

Basics.

Please forget what you've seen and heard on the TV and in movies for a moment. Those sources are for entertainment and promotion. Most often their content is false and thus bears little relation to the realities of gun selection, ownership and use.

What's the difference between a gun and a firearm?

None. Nothing. No difference. Those two words mean precisely the same thing, which is simply: a device intended to shoot (fire) projectiles from the open end of the barrel which is known as the muzzle.

Also: Please do not refer to guns as weapons. They are not weapons any more than a kitchen knife or a hammer is a weapon. They are devices or tools that can be used as weapons by anyone choosing to so use them. If you think about it, the person making that choice IS the WEAPON in that moment of use.

What is meant by pistol or handgun?

The words pistol and handgun mean the same thing. They refer to a gun (firearm) which is designed to be held and fired

The Beginner's Guide to Your First Handgun

in one hand, though both hands MAY be used to grip it at the user's option. Those are the defining comments.

In the current vernacular, many people seem to think that "pistol" means a particular type of pistol - usually a "semi-automatic". These seem most often to be the same folks that refer to a revolver (which is another type of pistol/handgun) as a 'cowboy gun'.

Don't let any of that confuse you? Breathe. Relax. Pay attention to this next bit. If you remember what comes next it can make things easier to grasp and remember. So here it is: ALL handguns ARE pistols. ALL pistols ARE handguns. Please read those last two sentences once more before moving on. Thanks.

Other word designations are merely ADDITIONAL information used to describe the particular device. Feel free to ignore the following little list of information until such time (possibly in the near future) that it matters to you.

Common Pistol/Handgun terms that people use (often incorrectly)

Revolver = Pistol = Handgun = Gun = Firearm
Semi-automatic = Pistol = Handgun = Gun = Firearm
Automatic (common but incorrect) = Pistol = Handgun = Gun = Firearm
Derringer = Pistol = Handgun = Gun = Firearm
Snubbie (or Snub-nosed) = Pistol = Handgun = Gun = Firearm
Mouse-gun = Pistol = Handgun = Gun = Firearm
Heater or Heat (slang) = Pistol = Handgun = Gun = Firearm

Do you see a pattern in this list? Please answer "Yes!"
For what it is worth, I most often use the word GUN when referring to any type of gun. Brilliant strategy on my part, eh? More specifically descriptive words are only used in this book

The Beginner's Guide to Your First Handgun

to clearly address a particular gun being discussed. But day-to-day, at home, at the shooting range, in classroom and instructional settings - GUN is THE word I'll most often use. I hope it'll become your word, too.

You want to choose the right handgun.

Good. I'm all for that. Which one is the right one for you? Before being able to help you find the right gun, there are a few things we'll need to establish, namely:

Nine Questions For Determining the Right Handgun (Necessary for success)
1) What is this gun going to be used for? (Target Shooting, Hunting, Personal Defense)
2) Where will it be used? (At the range, in the field, home defense)
3) By whom? (One or more persons)
4) How often? (Seldom, regularly, frequently)
5) How big are the hands of the person that will be using it? (Large, medium, small)
6) How strong and healthy are the hands of the person that will be using it? (Strong, medium, weak)
7) How mentally determined are you to continue with this? (Is it a whim or are you committed)
8) How much can you comfortably afford to spend on the gun AND the ammunition?
9) How does the gun feel in your hand?

When it comes to selecting which gun to buy, "**gun fit**" is the single most important consideration. **Gun fit** simply refers to the matching of certain characteristics of the gun to the corresponding characteristics of the shooter. Typically gun fit refers to physical traits of each, but let's not overlook other elements.

The Beginner's Guide to Your First Handgun

It is really difficult to accurately assign degrees of importance to the nine (9) questions in the list above. They are each very important. So the task before us is to find, as best we can, a gun that fits YOU best, YOUR circumstances best and YOUR pocketbook best.

The first eight of the nine questions can be answered at home, before you ever go shopping or read another article in a magazine. So let's tackle those right now and be very honest with your answers. I suggest you circle the choices that most accurately apply to you and your circumstances. **Then take it with you when you go shopping.**

What will this gun be used for? If you can be absolutely certain that this gun is only ever going to be used to shoot targets at a Shooting Range or similar safe set up in the yard, the selection process just became much easier. If it is for Hunting we will need to know which type(s) of game species will be hunted. If it is for Personal Defense it will be important to consider if that may be for inside the home, outside the home or both. (Go ahead and circle which choice(s) apply to you.)

Where will this gun be used? At the range. In the field. At home for defense. In the car. I plan to take it with me everywhere. (Circle the choices that apply)

Who will use this gun? Me and me alone. Me and my spouse/significant other. My whole family will be using this gun. (Circle the best choice)

How often or how much will this gun be used? Just while learning to handle it - then it goes into the sock drawer. I plan to become proficient and keep up my skills through regular practice. I can't wait to start shooting hundreds of rounds of ammunition every week. (Circle the best choice)

The Beginner's Guide to Your First Handgun

How big are the shooter's hands? Large. Medium. Small. [EXTREMELY IMPORTANT!] (Circle the best choice)

How strong and healthy are the shooter's hands? Strong. Medium. Weak. Healthy. Pretty good. I've got some challenges. (Circle one for strength and one for health)[EXTREMELY IMPORTANT]

How mentally determined are you to continue with this? Wild horses could not stop me. I'm reading this book aren't I? It seems like a good idea. Meh? (Circle one)

How much can you comfortably afford to spend? $1,000 or more; between $500 and $1,000; less than $500. (Pick the one that fits)

Your answers to the above can help a salesperson at the gun shop or sporting goods store as you shop. Even better, your answers from this above list will help determine which gun or guns would be the best ones for you to try out for fit and feel.

You will need to be willing to share the information about yourself from the above questions as you work through the next step in your quest. Which is:

Handling and Testing Different Guns for Gun Fit and Feel (#9 from the earlier list)

Handling - Before going further, let me say that you should <u>absolutely</u> handle any gun you are interested in acquiring for use before you proceed in the process. What do I mean and why? When I say you should handle the gun, I mean just that. Pick it up. Hold it. Aim it. Feel its weight, its heft. Too big, to small? How comfortably does it fit and feel in your hand?

It is extremely common for people to come to the range for advice or instruction already having a gun which is too large or too small for their hands. So understand this if you miss everything else: Hand size and hand strength contribute more to the overall success with a particular gun than any other factor. Why bring this up again? Because your happiness with your gun depends on it.   If self-defense is the intended purpose for this gun, your LIFE may depend on it. So I'm sincere when I tell you that the importance of this element in your involvement with guns cannot be overstated.

Test Firing - It will be best for you if you can test fire any gun before buying it. While it may not always be possible to do so, it is important enough that you should make a reasonable effort in this direction.

This does not need to be a difficult nor time consuming part of the selection process depending on where you live. If you are near a shooting range that rents handguns to shooters for use at the range, you should be able to narrow down your options to three or less very quickly. Such ranges are not in every town, but can most often be found using an Internet search or the yellow pages and then making some phone calls. If the person you are speaking with tells you that, "No, we do not have guns for test firing", be sure to ask if they know of a business or organization in your area who does. The shooting sports community is often quite friendly and welcoming to newcomers.

Check the 'net and the phone book. Make the phone calls. Take notes.

Alternatives to renting guns for test firing

When no stores or ranges in your area have guns for test firing or rental there are some other things you can do to accomplish this phase of your search.

Look for public or private shooting ranges to contact. Explain what you are trying to do.

The Beginner's Guide to Your First Handgun

Similarly, find a gun instructor to talk with and explain what you are trying to do.

Instructors and ranges should be able to offer to help you directly or put you in touch with someone who may be able to let you fire their gun or guns and help you with your decision.

The difference between sense and nonsense in advice that you'll hear

It will be necessary for you to seek some local advice. There are as many different opinions on these topics as there are people who'll give them. They CANNOT all be right. Put on your thinking cap when advice is flowing and pay attention the to the next few paragraphs. When I offer my advice or opinion, I'll back it up with logic or an anecdotal story, or, if you're really lucky - BOTH.

1) Advice regarding choice of caliber or cartridge: "Get the most powerful gun you can hold on to...Anything smaller just won't do the job or doesn't have enough stopping power, etc." We hear this one a lot from well-meaning but sometimes ill-informed friends or family. It is NONSENSE for at least three reasons. One being that we're talking about your first gun here and your experiences need to be somewhat pleasurable with it. Another reason being that if you don't practice A LOT with this gun you will never become proficient at handling, firing or hitting anything with it. More power equals greater recoil - which (for a beginner especially) reduces enjoyment and accuracy. The ammunition is usually more expensive as well. As for 'doing the job' or 'stopping power' I will now regale you with my first anecdote. Which goes like this: While enjoying an off-duty beverage with a couple of sailor friends one evening, we got into a discussion of which would be the best caliber rifle to use in a combat situation. A very senior Marine Gunnery Sergeant sitting nearby interjected his

opinion: "You Navy types with your deck-mounted cannon seem to think that the size of the bullet is all that matters. You're wrong. Only three (3) things matter: Shot placement, shot placement and shot placement." He was absolutely correct, because if you cannot hit what you are shooting at, it really does not matter what size projectile you miss with, now does it? Think about it.

2) Advice regarding choice of action - either revolver or semi-automatic: You will hear, "Revolvers are always more reliable, so get a revolver." NONSENSE. There are plenty of things that can go wrong with a revolver. And if they do, they are likely to be much more difficult to solve than with other guns. Conversely you may hear, "Get an automatic (semi-automatic) because you can shoot more rounds (shots) quickly than with a revolver." This is also NONSENSE.

3) Get the gun that you can most comfortably and confidently handle, shoot and clean and afford. Then learn to use it safely and practice with it regularly. That's my advice. You'll probably see this at least once more in this little book.

That's enough of that for now. It's time to go shopping! Or at least to decide where you'll shop.

Where to shop

Gun Stores (obviously)
Gun Ranges
Gun Shows
Sporting Goods Stores
Department Stores
Hardware Stores
Garage Sales
Classified Ads
Friends, Family and Acquaintances

The Beginner's Guide to Your First Handgun

Here are a few pro's and con's for each of those listed:

Gun Stores - pros: Since they specialize in selling guns, ammunition and accessories they are likely to have the widest selection all in one place. The good ones will have honest employees who know what they're talking about and who will be happy to answer questions. The best ones may be able to allow you to handle or even rent/test fire a few models if they have a range on premises.

Gun Ranges (we're only talking about those that sell guns) These usually only exist in medium to large city areas. They very widely in size and scope. The same comments that apply to Gun Stores apply here.

Gun Shows - pros: Depending on what part of the country they're in and who the promoters and sellers are, these can be the source of terrific deals on new and used guns and accessories. Pricing and specialized gear can be nearly unbelievable. cons: Every type of seller imaginable will be there which is NOT always good for beginners. You could be getting a great deal or you could be getting taken for a ride. Be careful and not in a hurry.

Sporting Good Stores - pros: Among the better known chain stores of this type you may find some of the best gear available along with good service and good advice. But be prepared to pay for it. cons: Not all of these will have merchandise within affordable reach of the less affluent buyer. If that includes you, prepare to leave empty-handed or with less change in your wallet than you had hoped.

Department Stores - pros: Assuming they sell handguns, they may have the lowest prices of any dealer. You will need to really know what you want, (because the) cons: Their employees tend to have very limited knowledge of the firearms they sell.

Hardware Stores - pros: Can save you a lot of windshield time if you are located in a very rural area. cons: Usually the selection will be quite limited.

Garage Sales - pros: You could run into the deal of a lifetime. cons: You could buy something totally unsafe, and there are no guarantees. As a beginner, avoid the Garage Sales unless you have a knowledgeable and trusted family member or friend who is assisting you.

Classified Ads - same comments apply as for Garage Sales.

Family, Friends and Acquaintances - cons: This can be the best or the worst group of all to purchase from or even get advice from. pros: If you are truly close to the person(s) AND they are experienced and knowledgeable they can be your greatest asset in finding the right first gun. You'll have to decide this before you ask for their help because once you do, there'll be no turning back without hard feelings. Notice that the pros and cons for this category have been reversed. Think about why that would be, please.

Brands, Models and Calibers

Some of you have been wondering when we would finally get around to this part of the selection process.

As explained earlier, I am not a gun salesperson nor dealer. I have no particular 'ax' to grind with any manufacturers. What follows are some very honest observations based upon personal experience (mine) - not what others have claimed. What you'll get here is either first-hand or the source will be identified.

The Beginner's Guide to Your First Handgun

Among the challenges of selecting the right gun is that fact that so many different makes (brands) exist. Most of them offer a wide selection of models (action, type, style, barrel length, color finish, weight and frame and grip configuration). Let's not forget how many different cartridges/calibers they might be designed to shoot. The sheer numbers of combinations to consider are at least stunning if not downright overwhelming.

Time for some good news: No one needs to consider ALL of these various options when seeking their first gun. Really. I promise. That is why it has taken until now to reach this point.

If you have diligently read and reviewed and filled out the Nine Questions earlier then you have already eliminated the majority of options for yourself. Then, taking that filled out list of attributes along, you will find that there will be a small number of guns available in the places you visit.

Carefully record the make, model, caliber and price of those guns which come closest to meeting the criteria established in the list of Nine. These will become your personal "Guns of Interest" list and you will reduce it to your own "Short List" fairly quickly.

Handling the ones on your "Guns of Interest" list will eliminate many if not most. (Handling as defined earlier in this chapter.) Once you have your "Short List" down to three (four at the most), it is time to try to test fire them all. That should be a major determining factor in the narrowing down process.

So then, you aren't going to comment on the Brands even?

Sure, since you insist. Kindly remember you asked for this, so bear along, 'kay?
50 and more years ago, virtually all cars driven in the US were manufactured here.

The Beginner's Guide to Your First Handgun

Much the same could be said for guns. Growth in manufacturing, marketing, transportation and even population shifts have changed all that. Look around at the cars for a second. Now let's go back to guns.

Colt makes some nice guns. So do Kimber, Smith & Wesson, Springfield, Remington and Ruger. Those are among the "big names" of US gun manufacturers. They've all been around for many decades and have big followings and produce very respectable guns. And the prices you'll be asked to pay for them reflect those facts.

There are many, many more manufacturers in the US making fine guns in a variety of styles, calibers and prices. They employ US residents and use US sources for their products. Some are owned by foreign corporations.

The US marketplace for guns is also home to more foreign made guns than US made ones. Plenty of them are great guns as well.

Uh oh. Now what? How do you finally choose the brand?

I try to follow these basic notions in finalizing my own brand selections:

a) Reputation of manufacturer and their written guarantee/warranty.
b) Reputation of seller and their repair or return policy.
c) Recommendation of seller <u>based upon YOUR criteria.</u> (You HAVE shown them your list, haven't you?)
d) Availability of the gun itself, ammunition and accessories.
e) Price of the gun, ammunition and accessories.

D and E above are intentionally placed at the end. d) Availability: If it is not available just now, find out if this is a temporary, cyclical or ongoing circumstance. Factor that in to your decision making. It may or may not be a deal breaker.

The Beginner's Guide to Your First Handgun

Your decision. e) Pricing is important for several reasons, among the most important of these is that you don't want to get stuck with a piece of junk that is dangerous to operate and cannot get serviced. Any new gun under about $275.00 (2015) would be very, very suspicious.

At the same time you do not need to pay exorbitantly just for a brand name. Always consider pricing together with the first two items (a and b).

But you didn't REALLY talk about calibers, either....

Quit whining. I did so talk about calibers. Remember the story about the Gunnery Sergeant?   It seems most folks want to start and center any discussion about gun selection on Caliber. This is nonsense when it heads in the direction of 'bigger is better', which it invariably does. **Get what you can handle and will practice with often**. And then make yourself proud.... Go out and PRACTICE with it. Get some training from someone who knows what they're doing.

Summary of this section:

Buy the gun that fits the bolded sentence in the paragraph above!

The Beginner's Guide to Your First Handgun

Handling Your First Handgun

A few words about gun SAFETY - in the home and elsewhere

Congratulations! You've gone ahead and done, it - bought your first ever handgun.
Oh boy, oh boy, oh boy! I hope you feel as good about it as I do.

Any time we have the opportunity to discuss handling the gun you will find me drawn to throw in an occasional word or two about **safety**. I'm fairly keen on the topic having managed to thrive these past decades without mishap in the presence of many guns by paying attention to **safety**. I would also like to point out that never in those several decades have I known even a single gun to initiate activity on its own. They always stay put, so put them **safely** someplace every time you handle them.

The first and cardinal rule for everything that follows is this: ALWAYS KEEP THE GUN POINTED IN A SAFE DIRECTION.

Even if everything else were to somehow go wrong, no one should be injured so long as you ALWAYS KEEP THE GUN POINTED IN A SAFE DIRECTION. While it will be up to you to figure out what is a safe direction in your own home, office, etc. - that safe direction will NEVER include innocent humans or pets.

The Beginner's Guide to Your First Handgun

Remember that bullets travel through walls and floors, so YOU MUST ALWAYS BE THINKING! Think about what is behind or outside that wall; what is above or below that ceiling or floor. Got all that?

If you can manage to ALWAYS KEEP THE GUN POINTED IN A SAFE DIRECTION, then the next thing to do is to START handling it. WITHOUT any live ammunition in the same room.

That's right. Handle the empty gun, without any ammunition present. This gets you familiar with the gun, how it feels, how it works. And it does so SAFELY. Get in the habit of treating it as though it is loaded. Most important in that treatment is as you've possibly already imagined ALWAYS KEEP THE GUN POINTED IN A SAFE DIRECTION.

I am amazed and encouraged at how quickly you are catching on. Please continue.

Practice as many of these operations as apply to your particular gun: opening the action, removing and inserting the magazine, opening and closing the cylinder, holstering and drawing from the holster. Remember, no ammunition at this time and (you guessed it): ALWAYS KEEP THE GUN POINTED IN A SAFE DIRECTION.

That was fun. Now set the gun down with the muzzle (business end of the barrel) pointed someplace safe. See there, I've already stopped shouting. Read the Owner's Manual. Study it. They're never very lengthy and will give you a wealth of knowledge about your gun, its safe operation, what type of ammunition to choose or avoid and how to clean and store your new purchase. Imagine that. A man recommending you read the Owner's Manual. Next thing you know I'll suggest using a map to find your way in unfamiliar geography.

The Beginner's Guide to Your First Handgun

When you've finished reading the owner's manual, make notes of anything that especially caught your attention on the first pass. Then in a couple of days go back and reread those sections. You'll retain it much better this way.

If you bought a used gun that did not have an owner's manual with it you can get one for it by searching on line. Most often the manufacturer will offer free downloads of the manual for your model gun on their website. Even if they don't, you should be able to find, download and print a copy for your make and model handgun. I strongly suggest you do so and then keep it with the gun.

Time to dispel another of the old, sacred myths of gun-lore: Never Dry Fire a Gun!

Malarky and balderdash, both very good words that have sadly fallen from wide use, are scarcely sufficient to express my contempt for this outdated notion. I would call it Bullsh*t, but then, this may be used in a family setting. One never knows while sitting at the keyboard just where their words will end up.

What is meant by "dry-firing"? Simply it is the act of firing the gun without live ammunition in it. It establishes a way to safely handle and practice with your gun while at home. No driving to the range, no paying for ammunition, no loud noises, no recoil, no cleaning afterwards. No muss and no fuss.

You still have to follow all the rules of safety and safe handling. NO LIVE AMMUNITION PRESENT IN THE SAME ROOM and ALWAYS KEEP THE GUN POINTED IN A SAFE DIRECTION. You may notice a pattern developing here. I certainly hope so.

For many decades we were told and taught that dry-firing ANY AND ALL guns was harmful to their mechanisms; particularly

The Beginner's Guide to Your First Handgun

the firing pins. Let's face it, without a firing pin your handgun is useless.

The good news is that this notion is mostly malarky and balderdash. It's just not true!
EXCEPT FOR ONE KNOWN EXCEPTION! .22 caliber semi-automatic rifles and (just to be safe) .22 caliber semi-automatic pistols. If your gun is one of these, DO NOT DRY FIRE IT until you learn otherwise from the gun's manufacturer. You will find either a warning in the Owner's Manual or a statement telling you not to worry about it. Instructions within a manufacturer-provided Owner's Manual for a specific gun supersede any general firing, loading or cleaning ideas shared in this guide.

The main idea to take from all this is that dry-firing is a perfectly acceptable practice for you and your gun in all but very few cases. As always, it is up to you to be responsible enough to find and apply the specific recommendation of the manufacturer and the follow it. Barring the manufacturer's specific prohibition against dry-firing a particular model of their gun, I support it for the reasons already given and a few more coming up.

Confidence, comfort, familiarity

I'm going to write following paragraph simply and withoutt my usual wisecracks. That's because I really want you to get it and lock it into your memory banks.

"Without becoming familiar with your gun, you will never become comfortable with it. If you never become comfortable with it, you will never attain your full confidence in using it that you would otherwise."

The Beginner's Guide to Your First Handgun

Do yourself a favor. Re-read the paragraph above this one. Slowly. Absorb it. Re-read it as many times as that takes. Why? Because once you have made your gun selection, the thought within those quotation marks underscores precisely how successful you will be in your relationship to YOUR GUN!

It is the most important single idea in this entire guide.

After all, how often do I quote AND bold my own writing?

Ammunition - The Good, the Bad and the Ugly

Good Ammo is Where you Find it - IMPORTANT

Ammunition is the stuff you feed your gun. It should be high quality and appropriate to the task at hand. It should be the right ammunition for your gun. Your gun will tell you what it wants to shoot, usually on the barrel or frame or chamber. Sometimes it'll tell you in more than one place. Some manufacturers will name particular brands of ammunition to use in their guns. Some will even specify brands to avoid. Please check your Owner's Manual again.

Ammunition from the store will come in a box clearly identifying the cartridge caliber and type, together with other good information. The cartridges themselves will be identified on the base, or headstamp. This headstamp comment is **not** true for rimfire cartridges (normally .22 caliber). Put on your glasses if need be, but make certain the ammo matches the gun being used. It can be hazardous to you and to others around you should you ignore this step.

Factory Loaded Ammunition

These come in colorful boxes, new from the manufacturer and will identify important aspects of the cartridges contained within. Caliber, cartridge length or other designation and bullet weight all usually appear clearly on the end flap of the carton. Other information such as muzzle velocity and muzzle energy may be present on the other surfaces of the carton. It's worth looking at this data.

Bullet Weight

Bullet weight is important mostly for comparative purposes as you develop an understanding and preference for one over another based upon your usage and experience. Starting with the lightest available weight may be your best option.

Muzzle Velocity and Muzzle Energy

As with bullet weight, muzzle velocity and muzzle energy are significant to consider as you learn more about as recoil and accuracy through use and practice with your gun. Lower muzzle speed and lower muzzle velocity equals less felt recoil. Start with the lower ones and work your way up as you see fit.

Factory Reloads

I strongly advise against buying or using Factory Reloads while you are a beginner in the shooting sports. You will learn more about ammunition as you progress along. Factory reloads are less expensive than new Factory ammunition, which is to be expected. Other complex considerations may enter in; thus my recommendation to avoid this while you are yet new and inexperienced.

Other Reloads and Handloads

These terms are meant to apply to all those cartridges that are loaded in private homes and garages and workshops by individuals.

There are as many different reasons for and types of reloading processes for modern metallic cartridges as there are people involved in that hobby. The vast majority of re-loaders are avid shooters first and reloaders second. Many got involved in

The Beginner's Guide to Your First Handgun

reloading as a means of saving money on ammunition, and this is still true today even if to a lesser degree.

Many reloaders are motivated by their own high standards of quality and accuracy. These types keep meticulous records of every cartridge they load. Others are not quite as particular. You cannot tell these people apart by looking at them.

It matters not which of the above categories a reloader or handloader might fit into. You cannot afford to use their ammunition at the early stage of your shooting experience because you assume all risk arising from shooting their ammunition. As you become more knowledgeable and experienced you may opt to make an individual decision which runs counter to this advice.

Safety First, Foremost and Always

The Big 3 - The NRA's Cardinal Rules of Gun Safety

What they are:

- ALWAYS KEEP THE GUN POINTED IN A SAFE DIRECTION
- ALWAYS KEEP YOUR FINGER OFF THE TRIGGER UNTIL READY TO SHOOT
- ALWAYS KEEP THE GUN UNLOADED UNTIL READY TO USE

If the <u>first rule of gun safety</u>: ALWAYS KEEP THE GUN POINTED IN A SAFE DIRECTION IS ADHERED TO, THE POSSIBILITY OF INJURY TO SELF OR OTHERS IS REDUCED GREATLY! SO IT IS THE MOST IMPORTANT RULE OF ALL TO FOLLOW AT ALL TIMES!

What they mean:

Simply enough: They say what they mean and mean what they say.

The Beginner's Guide to Your First Handgun

A person is expected to think and to apply good reasoning to all aspects of gun ownership, handling and use. So let's bring up the obvious approach to this.

As an example, a gun being used for hunting is considered pointed in a safe direction while being carried with the muzzle aiming downward. The same is true for a holstered handgun being carried for personal protection.

The RIGHT time to move the finger onto the trigger is after or as the target is acquired in the sight picture. NOT BEFORE.

The time to load the gun is just before it may become time to put a finger on the trigger. Think about that a minute. If going to the range for practice or into the field for hunting there is NO need to load my gun before arriving at either location, right? Loading the gun when it is on the shooting bench at the range makes sense - not before then. Loading the gun after entering the field (area) to be hunted makes sense, not inside the car, right?

What about a gun intended for personal defense? Realistically, so long as the owner of the gun has trained sufficiently to safely handle and load and shoot the gun then they should be responsible enough to carry it in a loaded condition - SAFELY. WHY? They have to keep their wits about them while carrying a loaded gun, because of its intended use. There would be no point to carrying an unloaded gun for protection. If the situation arises for the gun to be used, the threat causing that need is NOT going to pause while you load your gun. This is why military and police forces routinely carry loaded firearms.

Entire books have been written on this one topic alone. Suffice it for our purposes hear to state that **the gun will never cause a problem by itself. Therefore, all responsibility for carrying it and using it safely fall upon the owner.**

These rules and guidelines are meant to be observed by everyone, at all times and in all places.

Are there EVER exceptions?

As always, every rule must bump into an exception somewhere. When we get to the chapter and section on cleaning, we beef up the rule about not loading the gun to say:

NO LIVE AMMUNITION PRESENT IN THE ROOM WHILE CLEANING THE GUN. NONE. So the gun is empty. The chamber, the cylinder, the magazine(s) - All empty, checked and double checked. No boxes of ammo and no stray cartridges lying about. Also checked and double checked. This being the condition of the area in which we clean our guns, is there anyway the gun can go off? So when I look down the barrel of the gun after cleaning it thoroughly to inspect for any residue am I or anyone else in danger of being shot? I don't think so.

By the way, we've all heard the one about the guy who shot himself while cleaning his gun. Not if he followed what I just outlined above. No ammunition present means NO AMMUNITION PRESENT = No gun shot. Ever! NEVER! Okay.

You Decide the when and where

You must be in charge of the gun at all times to ensure SAFETY! If you make an exception to any safety rule at any time it should be a DECISION based on well-thought out and logical thinking. Since it will involve increased risk, it should be as TEMPORARY AND BRIEF AS POSSIBLE and be CONFINED TO A SPECIFIC LOCATION AND CIRCUMSTANCE. IT SHOULD NEVER OCCUR ACCIDENTALLY NOR THROUGH CARELESSNESS!

The Beginner's Guide to Your First Handgun

Shooting Your First Handgun

Finding the Best Teacher (Trainer, Instructor) for You

This section is where I try my darnedest to convince you that the best course of action at this stage of your shooting career is to find someone to teach you in person. This guide can do a lot, but my eyes cannot be on you, my ears cannot hear your questions and I cannot physically demonstrate things to you in person.

So please, please, please consider that getting a teacher (Instructor) is probably your best and safest and even least expensive option for your next few lessons. I'll even tell you some easy ways to find one or more and then pick the one that's right for you.

Why you might choose an NRA Certified Instructor

Whether or not you are personally familiar with the National Rifle Association or not really has no bearing on this decision. The point is that the NRA, more than any other organization, has been training citizens in the use of firearms since about

The Beginner's Guide to Your First Handgun

1872. They train and certify the Instructors and Coaches by training and certifying the Trainer Counselors.

None of these people are employed by the NRA by virtue of their certification(s). The Certification stands mostly to assure you that the person who holds it has had to undergo the same training course that they offer you and that they have convinced a third party, (in the case the NRA), of their qualification to do so.

In the most basic of the Instructor courses, each of us been exposed to a philosophy of teaching embraced by the NRA and the practical steps of setting-up, organizing and conducting classes. The philosophy as taught and tested neither encourages nor allows for dictatorships nor tyranny among the Instructor ranks.

<u>NRA Certified Instructors are all around and easy to find</u>

Believe it or not, this is absolutely true in the USA even if you are unaware of them. Last time I saw the published information there were nearly 100,000 NRA Certified Firearms Instructors in the United States and Canada.

This link to the NRA's main site will help you find instructors and courses in your area:
http://www.nrainstructors.org/Search.aspx . I suggest you use it to find a "NRA First Steps to Pistol Orientation" offered near a locale of your choosing. The course lasts about 4 hours, includes hands on firing instruction and will provide you with materials and information that you can use for years to come. It also reasonably priced. Though prices vary from place to place, ($50 on the low end to about $90 on the higher end), the small classes of 1 to 3 students as required by the NRA means you'll get personal help from a knowledgeable shooter. You'll also receive a nice certificate when you pass the course.

The Beginner's Guide to Your First Handgun

If there are no acceptable offerings of the First Steps Pistol orientation, you might search for the one titled, "NRA Basic Pistol Shooting Course". This is a longer, more intensive course lasting 8 or more hours including a written test. It will cost a little more than the First Steps Orientation, probably between $75 and $125 per person. The Basic Pistol classes are often scheduled for 8 or more students.

If you cannot find a class that works for you, try your local newspaper(s) classified ads or even display ads. Some Certified Instructors run ads giving contact information and some of them will include prices and schedules as they apply. Internet and/or Telephone Directory searches may turn up some leads. The Home Page for the NRA: http://home.nra.org/home might help. Be prepared to spend some time there; it's a big site with lots and lots of information.

You can and certainly should ask for names of reputable instructors from the place or persons where you purchased your gun. If you were willing to trust them for their recommendations and with your money, then you are probably willing to trust their advice in this matter as well.

Once you have a contact name or names, CALL THEM! Interview them on the phone. Don't waste their time and don't "grill them". Have your questions ready and written in front of you when you call. Be courteous and absolutely honest. Your interview should tell you a few important things about that person beyond their charges and availability.

Which things? Well, did they come across as surly, uptight, anxious or demanding? If so, you might wish to move on to another contact. Were they arrogant, obnoxious or dictatorial? Did they sound like someone you'd look forward to meeting in person?

Most Instructors of my acquaintance are truly decent people who like people and guns. Many of these, especially in the

The Beginner's Guide to Your First Handgun

less populated parts of the country, did not get into it for the money. If we had done so, we'd already have gotten out.

Select the Instructor you are most comfortable with based on the various ideas in the above paragraphs. Schedule you class. Go and learn to be safe and have fun with your gun learning the right way to load and shoot and clean it right from the start.

Why you might not choose an NRA Certified Instructor

Despite the truth stated above that there are nearly 100,000 such people in the US, the fact may be that none are located near you. Rare, but it happens.

Also, the best laid plans of mice and men oft go awry... Which is my way of misquoting Robert Burns to tell you that, since no system is perfect, a few dictators and tyrants do slip in, or develop over the years.

You might know or locate someone who is knowledgeable and willing to train you and it just happens that they're not Certified by the NRA. So what? Who they are and what they know and how they teach are more important criteria than who they've been certified by. Unless you are looking for some type of certification for yourself.

Summary of this section:

Find an Instructor or mentor of some sort.

If you absolutely cannot find someone suitable to teach you, then study the Loading, Unloading and Firing sections of the Owner's Manual for your gun. Take it with to the range. ALWAYS KEEPING THE GUN POINTED IN A SAFE DIRECTION ~AND~ ALWAYS KEEPING YOUR FINGER

OFF THE TRIGGER UNTIL READY TO SHOOT, go ahead and practice loading and unloading the gun.

If it becomes necessary to learn to shoot this gun without the above described help, the following information is intended to get you as safely through what comes next as possible.

Though it is not an ideal circumstance to learn shooting without a live person to teach you, it does happen. ALWAYS KEEPING THE GUN POINTED IN A SAFE DIRECTION, ~AND~ ALWAYS KEEPING YOUR FINGER OFF THE TRIGGER UNTIL READY TO SHOOT, ~AND~ ALWAYS KEEPING THE GUN UNLOADED UNTIL READY TO USE, go ahead and make your gun and yourself ready to shoot.

Following the instructions for shooting in the Owner's Manual for your gun, proceed at your own risk. This will include using a proper grip to control the gun. You should grip the handgun with your control hand, (whether right- or left-handed) and use your other hand (optional) in support of the control hand by wrapping the fingers around.

Go early and often, Grasshopper

When it comes to practicing, this is a simple bit of advice to give and it should be simple enough to follow. But folks ignore it. They become busy. Or distracted. Or bored.

Some may figure they've already learned it, so why bother. Short answer is that shooting well is a degradable skill (actually a number of skills combined). Unlike riding a bicycle, we do forget how to do it - especially how to do it well.

If personal defense is one of your reasons for having a gun in the first place, how much sense does it make to you not to be fully prepared to use your handgun when you need it most?

The Beginner's Guide to Your First Handgun

Take care of your eyes and ears, they're hard to fix or replace

The NRA recommends that everyone wear adequate eye protection and hearing protection. Most modern prescription lenses are sufficient should you happen to wear glasses. Some shooters prefer the soft sponge-type ear plugs made to be inserted; others like the ear muff or "cans" designs. Inexpensive shop glasses can be had at many store which will suffice in the beginning. You can upgrade to fancier equipment later if you are starting out on a limited budget.

How important is this protection? Several of the fellas I hunted with in my youth are deaf today or nearly so. None of us knew anything about hearing loss in those days. Though I've never met anyone who had vision problems arising from shooting activity it would only take one such incident for a person to be eternally convinced about the value of protective lenses.

Practice what I preach, but by all means PRACTICE

You can avoid boredom or drudgery in your handgun practice by merely incorporating some SAFE and creative variety into your routine. Makes it sound kinda like sex, I guess. That comment is meant for humor and NOT meant to recommend combining the activities of shooting guns and sex. In fact, consider this my total recommendation to NOT combine them.

<u>Try reactive targets.</u> Balloons react. Clay targets react. Exploding *targets react. *Please note that with exploding targets you will need to READ and FOLLOW the manufacturer's instructions completely. You will also need to obey the laws where you shoot regarding their use; claims that exploding targets can and have caused wildfires are not to be ignored. Also make sure that your range and the Range Safety Officer on duty have no objection to their use.

The Beginner's Guide to Your First Handgun

<u>Learn and practice a variety of shooting postures and grips</u>: Sitting - with or without a bench rest - both hands or one-handed. Standing - both hands and one-handed.

<u>Use a variety of static (non-reactive, non-exploding) targets</u> and vary the distance from your shooting position(s).

<u>Find a shooting partner or partners</u>, who are relatively nearby as well as being in a similar state of development as shooters go. Make sure that person is safe and that you share similar goals. It works especially well if you can challenge one another to grow and improve without becoming upset in the process.

<u>Find a mentor</u>, someone you can trust and learn from without going broke paying for lessons. Sometimes a former Instructor of yours will fill this role without charging for their time. Whoever it is, an occasional contribution to the gasoline or ammo fund is always welcomed even if not required or expected. *Wink, wink. Hint, hint* Especially so if they are retired folk. (There could be more hinting here, but I've decided to spare you that bit of joy.)

Maintaining, Cleaning and Storing

Break-In and beyond

As you read the Owner's Manual that came with your gun you should come across some mention of a breaking-in period. This is often expressed in a number of rounds (shots) fired. Many manufacturers will tell you that the gun will need to be fired several hundred times before reaching peak performance. A very few claim that their guns require no breaking-in. Believe what they tell you.

Some manufacturers will specify preferred ammunition and even name the brands and loads that function best in their guns. They might even specify a brand or two of ammunition NOT to be used.

Did I forget to mention reading the Owner's Manual earlier? In case you missed that part, I just mentioned it again.

Watching for the small changes

As you spend more time practicing with your gun you will learn to expect certain behaviors from it. Where the trigger 'breaks' or where it 'resets'. How it handles different types of ammunition. How much recoil it produces and so on.

Just as you would with raising a youngster, pay close attention, especially for changes.
Whether the changes are normal and expected, good or bad - no one will know the operation of your gun as well as you do.

Don't ignore changes that seem unsettling or cause you worry. If in doubt, take it to the gunsmith.

Have gunsmith - Will Travel

There never seem to be enough good gunsmiths around. Ask around for a referral and start with the one that you get referred to most. A really good one may be busy enough that they'll have a backlog of work. When you find a gunsmith you can get along with and does good work, treat them very, very well.

They can do much more than fix a broken gun, though they can often solve such a problem. You need to know that if you would like a different trigger pull, or release point or any number of other fine-tuning matters for your gun, a gunsmith can handle them for you. Usually for a reasonable price, as well.

Gunsmiths are like doctors anymore. They seldom travel to you.

Cleaning Your Gun - The Root of Much That is Good

Until now we've been mostly talking about the fun aspects of gun ownership. When it comes to cleaning, some among us just plain don't like it much. I had a brother like that once. He was an avid hunter and spent a lot of money on guns over the years. He never learned to enjoy cleaning them and was sometimes disappointed and frustrated when his dirty "shootin' iron" failed to go BANG when he wanted it to. He wasn't the only person of that persuasion that I ever ran into.

Until very recently I used all the old standard cleaning materials and products, If it was made by Hoppes or Outer's or Remington or Gunslick I had a bunch of it on hand and used it freely. I still use the Hoppes No.9, only these days I dab a little behind each ear as cologne because I still love the smell of it. It reminds me of the old days.

Whoever said that you, "Cannot teach an old dog new tricks" wasn't too far off. Once in while an old dog can fool you though. Lately, when it comes to cleaning my pistols I've been using a product called, **FrogLube**. I use their paste formula and can't say enough good about it. If you can't find it in a local store, look for it online. I happen to know that Amazon.com can ship you some. It lasts a long time because it only takes a little bit to do the whole job.

It is a 'C.L.P.' product, which means it **C**leans, **L**ubricates and **P**rotects. All in one operation. Instead of using three products, I use this one.

Rather than getting out a variety of tools and using upwards of 10 cleaning patches per pistol every time I cleaned them, I now use 2 or 3 disposable RAMRODZ, which look a bit like a glorified Q-Tip. They come sized to the caliber of your gun and are quite a bargain even if you have to pay for shipping.

Do it often and do it well

Especially when your gun is new, it should be cleaned every time you shoot, even if you only fire a few rounds through it.

Remember the break-in stage we talked about? A thorough cleaning with high quality products in the early life of your gun can help reduce that breaking-in process. Your gun will certainly perform better.

There's one more benefit from cleaning the gun early and well: You will really begin to know and respect and appreciate one another. This can be the beginning of a real relationship with a reliable friend, companion and partner. Or not. That choice is up to you.

Give Your Gun a Safe Home

You may recall that we talked earlier about handling and shooting the gun safely? Your gun will need a safe place to call home too.

Modern gun safes and security devices are affordable, convenient and readily available.
If you keep a loaded gun in the house for personal protection a safe is a wise and prudent investment. If you keep a loaded gun and have children around it becomes a necessity.

Except for that which is loaded in your personal defense gun, keep all ammunition stored apart from your gun(s). This is to avoid unauthorized persons from putting the two together and causing and accident or other problem.

The $2.99 Guide to Your First Handgun

A final disclaimer: Though I repeatedly mention the NRA and draw considerably upon their teachings and practices, nothing contained herein is to be construed as an endorsement by that organization. I am not now, nor have I ever been employed by the NRA.

I am a member of the NRA and think you should consider joining also. It is easy enough to do online and membership includes you choice from several excellent magazines about shooting and gun related issues.

The Author

Beginner's Guide to Your First Handgun

Thank you for buying this book. I hope you get as much from reading it as I did writing it.

All reviews are important to Authors. It is how we get found and how we improve. So before you leave this book I am asking you to give it your honest appraisal.

Made in the USA
Lexington, KY
13 May 2016